NATURE FIRST

NATURE FIRST

KEEPING OUR WILD PLACES AND WILD CREATURES WILD

BY THOMAS McNAMEE

Drawings by Susan Szeliga

ROBERTS RINEHART, INC. PUBLISHERS

The content of this book is based on remarks delivered
at the "Fate of the Grizzly" conference held at the
University of Colorado, Boulder, April 5, 1986.

For Frank Platt

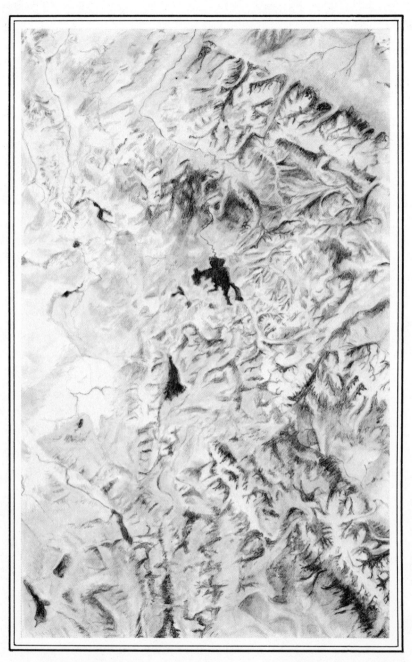

Greater Yellowstone

NATURE FIRST

Ask JANE Q. Citizen what comes to mind when she thinks about grizzly bears. I imagine two quite different pictures suggesting themselves: a), the adorable tussling cubs with their tender and vigilant mother; and b), a thousand pounds of gut-crunching terror ripping through the tent wall for a midnight snack of human flesh.

These two rather cartoonish images actually raise important questions about our culture's relationship to the bear, and perhaps to wildness in general. Why do we care so much about grizzly bears, and all they represent? And to express that caring, what should our aims be?

Grizzly bear conservation is different from other endangered species conservation. The grizzly exercises a unique power over the human imagination—it has a certain cachet which the Devil's Hole pupfish, say, seems to lack. In the admiring mind, and in the mind of his enemies too, the grizzly is not only real but also magical, and that peculiar magic is part of what we must deal with in grizzly conservation. In a scientifically ideal world, rare lichens, beetles, pond scum, and the dear old pupfish would get just as much attention as grizzly bears and Bengal tigers, but it doesn't work out that way. The great public ardor for the fate of the grizzly bears of the Yellowstone ecosystem, after all, concerns a population which, from a biological point of view, is relatively expendable. There are plenty of grizzlies in Alaska and Canada.

Nonetheless the Endangered Species Act of 1973 does specify that locally imperiled populations deserve protection too. It need not recognize the grizzly's "magic" to protect him, and it is equally obliged to the finny residents of Devil's Hole. It shines on bear and pupfish alike. The Endangered Species Act's great aim is no less than to conserve all forms of earthly life, irrespective of their cachet or lack thereof, wherever they are and in whoever's way they may stand. In the eyes of the Act, all species are equal. And that is why (even if its actual enforcement has proved to be rather less equitable than its vision) the

Endangered Species Act represents an important event in the history of Western culture: for while it is true that the justification for endangered species protection tends to be thought of largely in terms of those species' present or potential benefits to mankind, beneath the surface of the law there is also recognition of those species' right to exist regardless of their sentimental appeal or their utility.

And more is called for than just the preservation of species one by one. With the Endangered Species Act and the view of nature it represents, we are concerned with more than just the preservation of genetic material. Otherwise, zoos and greenhouses and arboretums and seed banks might suffice us, and we could save the billions of dollars we've spent on national parks, wildernesses, wildlife refuges, critical habitat, and so on, and put all that land and all that money to "productive" use. Yet of course that's inconceivable—because what we care so much about is not just individual species, but the whole natural world they are part of. We care about what it is, and how it works, because it is our ancestral home and because it is the repository of biological knowhow, even wisdom.

The very word *conservation* implies a fear that we may lose that world, and it is surely no accident that our modern sense of the word dates to the first urban pollution of the River Thames. Humanity swarms over the landscape and changes it for its own use, and suddenly people find themselves missing the unuseful Eden from which their craving for dominion has expelled them. The worship of forest and water and sunshine and animals becomes a kind of nostalgia, a desperate hanging on— conservation. But conservation of what, exactly?

I believe that the true object of conservation is *nature*. This may sound
simpled-mindedly obvious, but if you
think about it hard it gets complicated
fast. What *is* nature? Our conception of
it springs from the darkest depths of our
unconscious sense of life itself, and an-
cient irrational urges and fears give it its
power, but at the same time, because
we pride ourselves on reason, we also
invest nature with an objective, ra-
tional, manageable, thinkable value.

Sometimes the mythic attributes of a
wild creature and its objective value
come into conflict as our culture
evolves. I immediately think of snakes
and wolves, and how they have tradi-
tionally been seen as repugnant. More
recently, however, they have become
dear to the hearts of millions of school-
children. When, like that, the myth and
the reality converge, then you are near-
ing the source of the meaning of nature.

And it is owing to just such a convergence, I think, that so many of us get so
worked up about grizzly bears.

Jane Q. Citizen's mythic images of
the fuzzy frolicsome teddies and their
solicitous mother and of the terrifyingly
unpredictable man-eater are powerful
because they happen to be objectively
true. Grizzlies *are* wonderful mothers;
grizzly cubs *are* the epitome of fun; and
grizzlies *do* sometimes attack and even
eat people.

Nothing artificial can summon up precisely this kind of emotional power. I
say, nothing *artificial.* Nothing "made
by man, rather than occurring in nature" (*American Heritage Dictionary,*
1969). This brings us another step
closer. Nature is not artificial: the hand
of man is excluded from it. Shall we say
then that a cow and a cowpasture are
not natural, but a deer and a woods are?
That sounds reasonable.

But what if the forest has been planted by man? What if the deer is there by dint of reintroduction of an ex-tirpated population? And what about man himself? Aren't we part of nature too?

Now it starts to get complicated, and we have to distinguish among varying versions of nature—for instance, "the physical world, usually the outdoors, in-cluding all living things." Well, we hu-mans are certainly includable among all living things, but do we have to live outdoors? You see, even the dictionary gets confused about this issue.

Another definition of nature is "the primitive state of existence, untouched and uninfluenced by civilization or artificiality." Yet most of us sense that somehow a woods full of deer—even a managed woodlot with reintroduced deer—or for that matter a backyard garden—really ought to be seen as in some way part of nature too. After all, still another of my trusty dictionary's definitions of nature is "the forces or processes of the physical world," and certainly woodlots and deer and gardens do embody those forces and processes.

This sort of ambiguity in our conceptions of nature permeates the dialogue about how natural ecosystems and wild creatures should be treated, and before we can return to Yellowstone and grizzly bears, we need a working definition of nature in its specifically conservationist usage.

Our definition should exclude unwieldy generalizations like "all living things" and vague jargon like "the outdoors." It should try to focus on an essence. What seems to me essential in the conservationist idea of nature is *wildness*—wildness not just of individual organisms but of places, situations, processes, ecosystems. A wild creature removed from its wild context is no longer wild, no longer natural: a lion in a cage, a fern in a pot, is not nature.

For a definition of nature specifically as the object of conservation let me pro-pose the following: *all those living things and all those biological forces and processes which are largely untouched by civilization or artificiality.*

What is crucial in this definition is the exclusion of the forces of civilization—that is to say, the idea of wildness. Thus an Amazonian Indian still living the old hunting-and-gathering life *is* a part of nature, but you and I are not. The cow, bred by genera-tions of artifice, and the cowpasture, fenced and maintained by man, are then, strictly speaking, not natural.

And what about the reintroduced deer and the woodlot? I suppose you could vote to include them, on the grounds of our definition's inclusion of

natural *processes* untouched by civilization or artificiality. Man has made the
conditions of their growth possible, but
the processes of forest succession and
the breeding and foraging of the deer
take place largely untouched by artifice—that is, they may owe their existence to man, but their *behavior* is natural. Even while including the deer and
the woodlot, however, I think we must
keep in mind that doing so has been a
compromise, and that many more such
compromises would soon land us en-
tirely outside of our definition. Suppose,
for example, we introduce an aggressive
tree-thinning timber harvest, and we
shoot ninety percent of the buck deer
every fall, or we sterilize them to keep
the population stable. Are we then still
within the pale of nature?

There are many such ambiguously
"natural" situations in our world, and
about them there will inevitably be

disagreement. But our society's very evi-
dent passion for real wilderness, where
the hand of man is either absent or in-
visible, shows that compromised nature
of the woodlot-and-deer variety does
not meet all our needs. Alpine Switzerland is a gorgeous place, but can that
pastoral landscape stir the heart as
deeply as an Alaskan valley whose scen-
ery may be much like Switzerland's but
where two hundred thousand caribou
crash across a roaring, undammed river?
I think not. And it is precisely the awe-
some naturalness of the Alaskan scene
that gives it its resonance. You might
add some Inuit subsistence hunters to
the picture, and maybe even a backpack-
er's tent or two, but if you add a ski
resort and kill off the caribou, well, you
might as well go to Switzerland, where
you can eat foie gras at Girardet's at the
end of your hike.

Now LET'S
think about what we have that fits our
definition of nature here in the lower
forty-eight United States. Most of it
falls somewhere between the mountain
pastures of Switzerland and the savage
splendor of Alaska, and over the years
we have jury-rigged a system of classifi-
cation that fits the picture not at all
badly.

In my little brick-walled back yard in
New York City's Greenwich Village, I
have bluejays, starlings, crows, doves,
house finches, pigeons, several kinds of
sparrows, various migrating birds in sea-
son, squirrels, mice, my cat Elvis, En-
glish ivy, azaleas, a few very tolerant
annuals, and a climbing rose. Every
morning and evening, thousands of
seagulls pass over through my little
square slice of sky, commuting to and
from the garbage dumps. Once, last fall,
a raptor, perhaps even one of the two or
three peregrine falcons that have been
hacked on New York skyscrapers and
bridges, swept down on a pigeon
beneath my birdfeeder (and missed, by
the way). In Central Park, I hear from
my excited friends on the Upper East
Side, there is now a small but reproduc-
ing population of raccoons. This, I
guess, makes a pretty good rock-bottom
limit for the most compromised possible

definition of nature, and I imagine that by most people's standards it doesn't qualify at all.

Right next to John F. Kennedy airport, still within the New York city limits, is the Jamaica Bay Wildlife Refuge. You can see the skyline of Manhattan from it, glittering black against the red hydrocarbon sunset, and out across the salt marshes to the edge of the bay, as the 747s thunder overhead, you can also see thousands of flapping, honking shorebirds, all just as obliviously content as if this were the fifteenth century. Is this nature? At one end of the spectrum, I suppose, it is.

On through our American categories, we have the sort of state parks where picnicking with the ants and the chipmunks is probably the primary mode of contact with nature. There are also the sort of wildlife refuges whose principal aim is the production of waterfowl for sport hunting, and the kind of national forests, seen most often in the South-east, where "nature" seems to function mainly as a wood factory.

Beyond these we come to the more typical national forests, where one of many "multiple use" management goals is at least an impression of naturalness —to the extent that such an impression can be maintained while also providing for timber harvest, mining, livestock grazing, oil and gas production, hunting, fishing, trapping, horseback riding, back-packing, off-road vehicle use, motorcy-cle racing, snowmobiling, downhill ski-ing, water skiing, resort development, road building, volleyball, and a few hundred other expressions of human na-ture.

Further up the scale, we find classified wilderness. In it, wildness is supposed to be the primary goal of management. Even here, however, some human activities result in significant compromises, such as sport hunting, which changes both the numbers and the behavior of game animals, ulti- mately also affecting other animal species, plant populations, and soils. The Wilderness Act of 1964, under which these lands are protected, allows an astonishing array of other intrusions as well—mining, for example, if you can imagine.

Finally we come to the national parks. Our greatest national parks en- compass vast tracts of magnificent wild country, and in them alone is it possible to make the conservation of nature the dominant value. It is pleasant to be able to report that, albeit by fits and starts and with a few shocking exceptions, the National Park Service has over the past fifteen years or so been moving toward exactly that—proclaiming nature con- servation as its central ideal. The Park

Service is also obligated to provide for human use and enjoyment, but their assumption increasingly has been that enhancing naturalness also enhances human enjoyment of the parks.

Even while taking such a righteous theoretical stand, however, the Park Service's actual practice has, as I've said, occasionally fallen from the path of naturalness. There is a gargantuan hotel complex called Grant Village now under construction in Yellowstone National Park, for example, that makes a mockery of the natural wonder in which it floats like a you-know-what in the punchbowl.

Of course, running national parks in the real world isn't easy. Beneath every bridge the Park Service must cross, there lurks, like a troll, some politician with a drawn bow and a quiver full of budget cuts, restructuring threats, and reassignments to latrine duty at the Podunk National Roadside Area.

Even without political interference, perfect naturalness is no more achiev-able in the national parks than perfect justice is possible in the courts. But that is not the same as to say that natural-ness is an invalid goal. Somewhere, we must have a benchmark, a standard, a governing principle. Somewhere, in all our artificial and semi-natural world of factories and automobiles and cowpas-tures and woodlots, we must have places where the conservation of nature is paramount.

Let's consider what that means in terms of real-life national park and wil-derness management. Here, as in the im-ages with which this discussion began, the convergence of myth and reason is critical. What is "natural" in the depths of the collective unconscious and what is "natural" according to the under-standing of science have an opportunity to coincide in our greatest national parks and wildernesses. They can be treasuries not only of human awe but also of biological processes free of human influence: they can be cathedrals and laboratories at the same time. In these great wild places, as almost nowhere else in the modern world, the religious impulse and the urge to understand can live comfortably together. And to whatever extent the naturalness of a wild place is degraded, both the spiritual experience of it and the scientific experience inevitably suffer.

The greatest obstacle to nature conservation in the national parks and wildernesses, far more significant than their management policies, is the disparity between official boundaries and biological ones. When most of these reserves were created, ecology was not exactly a household word, and the idea of enclosing self-sustaining ecosystems never entered the minds of the national parks' and national forests' creators. The result is that with very few exceptions our officially protected wild areas are incapable of conserving nature on the large scale necessary for the free play of natural forces. Many of those parks and wildernesses which have succeeded so far in preserving their natural condition may have done so not so much because of official protection as because most of the surrounding land has been too inaccessible or too poor to be deemed worthy of development. New technologies have made remoteness and low resource quality much less of an obstacle to development, however, and thus many supposedly protected lands are now severely threatened.

Yellowstone National Park is at the heart of one of the most pristinely natural areas in the United States, and yet it is also laced with roads, festooned with big hotels, and ecologically continuous with national forests of varying degrees of naturalness and *non*naturalness which are in turn contiguous to ranch-lands and towns. Yellowstone Park is visited by about two million people a year, most of them in the brief summer when most of the resident organisms must do most of their growing. How can this possibly be treated as *natural*?

Well, thank God for the resilience of nature—for even after a century of modern human use and misuse, Yellow-stone remains remarkably healthy. And why? Because the *forces* and the *processes* of nature have remained largely intact there, as is the case hardly anywhere else in the Lower Forty-eight. The hotels, the roads, the hordes of cars and tourists, and the hunters who swarm through the surrounding na-tional forests every fall have not irrepar-ably damaged the natural systems of Yellowstone.

Which is by no means to say that there has been no damage. The wolf is extinct, wiped out sixty years ago by a government extermination campaign. The numbers of cougars and wolverines may be unnaturally low and not recovering. Whooping cranes and peregrine falcons are critically rare. Many of the area's waters have been taken over by nonnative fish species. And the grizzly bear population has been declining for twenty years, and is decidedly in trouble.

Nevertheless the naturalness of this ecosystem is extraordinarily pure, even given its pollutants. And the means to its further purification can be clearly visualized through the lens of purer naturalness. Personally, I would love to see the Yellowstone area's national forests absorbed by the national park, or at least have all extractive use banned from the ecosystem, including

hunting—not because I object to hunting but because I think there ought to
be some magnificent ecosystem somewhere where all the constituent organisms' populations are naturally regu-
lated, and Yellowstone seems like the
best place imaginable for such an experi-
ment. But forget it—it won't happen, at
least in the foreseeable future. Within
the range of the feasible, however, there
is a great deal that can be done to increase the naturalness not just of Yellowstone National Park but of the en-
tire Greater Yellowstone ecosystem.

That's an important point right there.
Although human influence will obvi-
ously never be excluded from this
ecosystem, it *is* an ecosystem. The national park alone can never maintain
natural animal populations: it's a high-
elevation plateau, much of it suitable
only as summer habitat, and it amounts
to only about forty percent of the Yel-

lowstone ecosystem as a whole. So, before very many of my improvements
really become feasible, the ecosystem
must be thought about as such. There is
progress along this line—there is better
coordination among the various land
management agencies than there has
ever been before—but there's still a
very long way to go, and at least in the
Forest Service, there is not yet even
unanimous recognition of the inherent
interdependence of Yellowstone's natural systems. Meanwhile, the threats to
Yellowstone's continued naturalness are
piling up apace. The Greater Yellowstone Coalition has compiled a fat in-
ventory of these threats, and it makes
for truly harrowing reading: poaching,
mining, logging, new roads, ski resorts,
oil wells, dams, geothermal development, subdivisions . . . augh!

Yellowstone, frankly, has been damned lucky so far. The Greater Yellowstone ecosystem is so huge and so remote that it has been insulated from degradations nibbling at its edges, and although what passes for unified ecosystem management has been essentially seat-of-the-pants flying—managers making their decisions intuitively, according to what feels right—the human intuition for naturalness is pretty strong, and a lot of the managers' decisions have been good. Of course, there are still plenty of bad decisions. The disharmony of the area's recently released national forest plans, for example, is striking. A new interjurisdictional committee of land managers has been set up, however, and we'll see if they do better. The best they will be able to do, sad to say, is to make things less bad (rather than better), because the Forest Service's mandate for commodity output

makes it virtually impossible to imple-
ment ecosystem protection comprehen-
sive enough to be meaningful.

If administrators could simply put the
conservation of nature first, and where
possible the restoration of nature, then
their ecosystem management decisions
would fall neatly into place. Admit-
tedly, sometimes the action dictated by
that principle might not be possible, but
at least you'd have a baseline. The prob-
lem is that under the existing jurisdictions, only the national parks can really
put nature first. For them at least, nature first can be an effective guiding
principle. Thus:

Concessioner wants to put in tennis
courts at Roosevelt Lodge? Hell, no.
Wolves extinct? Reintroduce them, feed
them in a pen until they're oriented,
then release them and leave them alone.
(In the case of wolves, you also have to
protect livestock in the adjoining

private lands, and a good management system has already been proposed in the Rocky Mountain Wolf Recovery Plan, with a fully natural central zone, a buffer zone around it in which natural-ness is maintained as long as wolves aren't extending their range too far out-ward, and a final outer zone in which depredating wolves can be either relo-cated or killed. You might say then that we will have an artificial wall around a natural ecosystem—a necessary compro-mise in the protection of wildlands al-most everywhere today.)

Grizzly population declining? No, you don't feed them to try to increase their reproductive rate or lure them into den-sities greater than is historically natural in the Yellowstone ecosystem. Among the numerous unnatural behaviors artificial feeding would be likely to foster could well be a loss of natural food-gathering skills and a concomitantly greater likelihood of a grizzly bear assault on human food sources if the artificial feeding were ever stopped—precisely what happened when the Park Service closed the old garbage dumps in Yellowstone in the late 1960s. Artificial feeding has also been closely linked to increased aggression against people; for a full discussion, see Stephen Herrero's book *Bear Attacks*.

The main reason for the Yellowstone grizzly population's continuing decline is another sort of strong unnatural influence on bear life, in the form of bullets. If you suppress the killing of Yellowstone grizzlies by humans, the population will almost certainly recover. In the meantime, to whatever extent man-caused mortality continued, wild grizzlies could be brought in from somewhere where there are plenty, like Canada.

Unnatural, you may say, this sort of compensation? Well, yes, short-term. But the long-term result would be a continuing *wild* population of grizzly bears, independent of further human meddling. The essential quality of grizzly bears—their *wildness*—would be preserved.

And what about research?—all those traps and drugs and helicopters and rangers and biologists intruding on the poor bears' ever-shrinking privacy. Here again, I think, we have a minor violation of naturalness for the sake of a far greater enhancement of it. We must know the grizzly bear; we must try to know what it means to be one—because we cannot keep the grizzly's world wild unless we understand what makes it so. We must know that the whitebark pine nut crop is critical to Yellowstone grizzlies' nutrition, the huckleberries to those of Glacier. We must know where grizzlies mate, where they raise their cubs, where they den for the winter. We must know which human activities they will tolerate and which will send them fleeing. We must know—as we are now learning—how purely natural the grizzly's habitat must be to support a wild, free-ranging, self-sustaining population. And we must know if the population is in fact sustaining itself.

None of this is possible without radio collaring, and radio collaring is not possible without trapping and tranquilizing. The question researchers must always ask themselves is, Is our work compromising the naturalness of our subject? If phencyclidine hydrochloride really turned grizzlies into crazed killers, I would say let's drop it right now. But it doesn't. Indeed the effect of current research techniques on natural grizzly bear behavior seems almost nil. It would be nice if the biologists didn't occasionally kill bears with drug overdoses, but such accidents seem unfortunately to be part of the price of doing business. And given the death rate so far from such causes, the cost/benefit ratio is still quite strongly in the grizzly bear's favor.

If we can agree now that a worthy goal for Yellowstone is an ecosystem that can harbor in perpetuity a self-sustaining, free-ranging, *wild, natural* population of grizzly bears, we must ask whether our current conservation strategies can really achieve it. We must ask whether our strategies take into account three *natures* in yet another sense of the word—that is, "the intrinsic characteristics and qualities of a person or thing"—namely, human nature, the nature of institutions, and the nature of the grizzly bear.

Bear nature, of course, is what bear research is all about, and splendid progress has been made in the last twenty years. Indeed we probably understand ursine behavior better than human or institutional.

The nature of institutions is hard to know, but the study of it is a growing and fertile science. Bear conservationists would probably do well to bring in some good systems analysis. One of the things I most admire about the current Yellowstone grizzly management guidelines is that they attempt to set up an institutional structure that will work more or less regardless of who has what job—just as a systems analyst would like. Nevertheless we still see a lot of variation in the individuals charged with saving the Yellowstone grizzly.

The conservation groups most active on Yellowstone's behalf—the National Audubon Society, Defenders of Wildlife, and the Greater Yellowstone Coalition—have all shown themselves to be acutely aware of the difficulty of getting institutions and their personnel to live up to their proclaimed goals, and they have pushed and pulled and prodded the agencies as intuition and sympathy have dictated. This, to me, seems like really significant progress. Confronta-

tion has been superseded by cooperation. Managers, researchers, conservationists, and sometimes even developers
and ranchers can sit down together
with more or less common assumptions
and goals. And of course such a strategy
is rather more likely to get results than
name-calling and vitriol, of which in recent times there have been plenty.

Another important development has
been the establishment of the Inter-
agency Grizzly Bear Committee, which
brings together on a regular basis the ex-
ecutives of all the federal and state
agencies involved in grizzly recovery.
The big advantage here has been the in-
volvement of high-level decision makers,
who understand the intricacies of getting the committee's initiatives actually
carried out.

Even amidst such admirable institutional progress, however, human nature
insidiously intrudes. Are the conserva-

tionists now in bed with the bureau-
crats? Sometimes this worries me. They
spend all these hours together, agreeing
on mutually acceptable terms, forging
common goals, getting to know one
another, drinking beer, being pals—in
short, getting very deeply invested in
the conclusions they all come to together. Does this make the conservationists lose perspective? Is too much
cooperation a bad thing? I don't
know—I just raise the question.

And I worry about everybody getting
embroiled in *proceduralism.* Sometimes
these heroic conservation strategies look
wonderful on paper and rather less good
in the field. Far too many managers look
only at the input—their initiatives,
their rules, their procedures, their good
intentions—and assume that the output
will conform to expectations. Look at
the Yellowstone guidelines' provisions
for preventing illegal killing of grizzlies,

for example, and then look at what happened in the fall of 1985 in the Bridger-Teton National Forest. They seem like two different universes: on one hand, strict guidelines, clean camps, the law; on the other, to hell with the guidelines, filthy camps, anarchy, and four dead grizzly bears.

The point here is twofold: that many of these brave initiatives *may* bear fruit as long as good will and good faith are maintained; and that many of our brave initiatives are in fact, even now, not bearing fruit at all. The conflicts engendered by the inherent opposition of conservation and natural resource development are likely to get more strident as times goes by—good faith and good will, in short, will probably grow scarcer yet—and in any case the wilderness we have left will not admit of much more compromise. As we have seen, much-compromised nature very quickly becomes not-nature.

Moreover, we are losing bits of wild nature every day. The U.S. Forest Service and the Bureau of Land Management, among others, are dedicated to multiple uses of the land, of which nature conservation is only one; such is their legal mandate, and such too is their mind-set. Yes, their goals *include* conservation, but where it is not compatible with other objectives like commodity output, conservation often loses out. When conservation wins, it is usually thanks to the good will of some nice person who has found a way to do the right thing without jeopardizing his career. But must conservation rely forever on the charity of individuals? When bad times come (and come they always do, as time goes by), charity tends to dry up.

Each jurisdiction makes its own decisions, and nobody adds up the cumulative price. The result has been a wild acceleration of demands on ecosystem resources. Huge resort developments are under consideration all around Yellow-stone. A number of timber sales will require new roads, which are among the worst things you can do to grizzlies and are harmful to many other species too: many wild animals, including elk and especially grizzly bears, tend to keep well away from roads, because of the trouble (in human form) roads tend to bring; thus these roads irreparably fracture what has been unbroken wildlife habitat, and the inevitable result is reduced populations.

Oil exploration is under way in much of the area, without any consideration of the effects of later extraction. A good bit of de facto wilderness is not officially designated and is therefore still vulnerable to all sorts of exploitation. Hydroelectric projects; geothermal energy development; mining; poaching;

livestock (with sometimes trigger-happy owners); garbage and other attractants that lure bears into fatal encounters with humans; etc. ad nauseam—can we really hope that high-minded committees can keep all this from doing brutal damage to the natural condition of Yellowstone? There are noble battles being waged against virtually all the threats to the Yellowstone ecosystem, but if you stand back and look at the big picture, you will see that nature is losing the war. Many of our other wildlands are in similarly perilous straits.

It is human nature, alas, not to see the big picture. How often do managers or researchers or even the involved conservationists envision the course of grizzly bear life over the last century and into the century beyond? It makes for a supremely depressing vision, and it makes our supposedly heroic efforts look small indeed. Such enormous human

forces are arrayed against the bear—
population growth, the hunger for energy and raw materials, the expansion of
leisure time, the alienation of our citi-
zens from natural processes, the attri-
tion of wildness worldwide. The mind
reels, with helplessness, even despair.

Yet as those human forces advance,
grizzly bears and all they represent become more precious. The greater the
reach of civilization and artificiality, the
greater the need for nature and wildness.

How shall we address that ever-
growing need? I believe that our current
jury-rigged system of nature conservation, although it has served us well in
the past, will not be sufficient to
preserve our greatest wild ecosystems in
the future. Much of the chaos in Yellowstone can be attributed to the
hydra-headed ownership of the ecosystem and all the administrative con-

trariety that that entails. I am told that we cannot hope to change the present snarl of jurisdictions. It's politically im-possible. But there is something else we can do.

I PROPOSE THAT we establish a system of National Biosphere Reserves. The United Nations' International Biosphere Reserves program provides a ready and excellent precedent for the defining of such entities, but it has no force in American law, and American parks designated as International Biosphere Reserves have often been unable to live up to the definition. (Yellowstone National Park, for example, is already an I.B.R., but the ecosystem as a whole is not—with all the consequences outlined above.) For a national system to work, it would have to be written into law.

As I envision them, National Biosphere Reserves would have three principal characteristics:

1. nature conservation would be the primary goal of land management;
2. existing jurisdictions would be maintained;
3. and the National Biosphere Reserve designation would be advantageous to the human communities affected.

Thus, in a Yellowstone National Biosphere Reserve, there would still be Yellowstone National Park and Grand Teton National Park; all or part of the Gallatin, Custer, Shoshone, Bridger-

Teton, Targhee, Caribou, and Beaver-
head national forests; the John D.
Rockefeller, Jr., Memorial Parkway; the
Red Rock Lakes National Wildlife Refuge and the National Elk Refuge; Bureau of Land Management lands; Bureau of Reclamation lands; state lands of
Idaho, Montana, and Wyoming; parts
of sixteen counties in those three states;
and private lands. Each unit of public
land could still be managed as such but
would be accountable to some guiding
authority, perhaps a chief executive
selected by the constituent agencies.
With meaningful incentives (and hence
on a strictly voluntary basis), the
private lands could be managed through
a land trust acting in consultation with
the public lands authority.

The major difference in land management would be that under the National
Biosphere Reserve policy of nature first,
the government agencies' old ways of

doing business would have to be good for the ecosystem as a whole or else be changed. The Forest Service, for example, could be freed from some of its present commodity output requirements, and the Park Service could structure recreation and related development in ways that harmonized with the fundamental ideal of nature conservation.

Private lands could receive tax benefits or other inducements to protect their natural character, while continuing with ranching or other commercial activities. Local communities (such as Dubois, Wyoming, which has suffered greatly from recent reductions of timber harvest) could receive financial aid, job training, and other benefits as their economies shifted toward tourism, research, recreation, and other nonextractive industry. Far too often, residents and neighbors of wild ecosystems have had to pay a high price for the satisfaction of national conservation constituencies. Profits have tended to go elsewhere, while the local people get the crumbs under the table. National Biosphere Reserves should encourage local ownership and local benefit.

Most important, National Biosphere Reserves would insure the preservation of some of the planet's most precious natural treasures. Under the present system of supposedly perpetual protection, many of our national parks and wilderness are simply not safe, either in perpetuity or even in the short term. We have very much still to learn from the processes of nature, very much still to gain—material benefits, spiritual benefits, knowledge, understanding, perhaps even wisdom.

A system of National Biosphere Reserves in the United States might in turn inspire similar approaches in other nations. Many of the world's most valuable wild ecosystems are plagued by multijurisdictional conflicts precisely analogous to those in the Greater Yellowstone area. By providing a model for the cooperation of existing management agencies, and demonstrating that such cooperation can promote both the ecological and the economic health of the designated regions, the creation of a system of American National Biosphere Reserves might in the twenty-first century be considered an event as significant as the creation of the first national parks in the nineteenth century seems now, in the twentieth. And what better first National Biosphere Reserve could there be than the ecosystem centered on the United States' (and the world's) first national park, Yellowstone?

Two ocean

Plateau is a big flat-topped mountain in the remote headwaters of the Yellow-stone River. Most of the plateau lies outside the national park, in the Bridger-Teton National Forest. It's hard to get there even in summer, twenty-some miles in from the nearest road and a long climb up, but then once you reach ten thousand feet, the landscape is an open, easy, grassy stroll, like a golf course—scattered islands of trees, crescents of snow, sun-dazzled lakes, an endless unrolling of flowers, no need for a trail. You can see the Tetons, Yellowstone Lake, the Madison Range, the Gallatins, the Absarokas, the Wind Rivers, miles and miles of miles and miles. Except for a surveyor's benchmark in a cairn at the crest and a footbridge over the river far below, you cannot see a sign of man.

Two Ocean Plateau has always been a very popular place with Yellowstone's grizzlies: there are spawning trout in the streams, swales of succulent forbs, groves of nut-rich whitebark pine, plenty of pocket gophers, marmots, and elk to prey on. Plenty of solitude. Some day soon, it may also be a good place for a wolf pack.

Here, for centuries, the same particolored lichens have grown on this

same black volcanic rock. Summer after summer, the same wildflowers have bloomed in its crevices. This grass has been cropped every year by the same elk herd. Fires have swept through—you can see the blackened lodgepole pines here and there on its flanks, and resurgent green beneath. The Yellowstone caldera has erupted from time to time, burying Two Ocean in hot ash, pushing it up or knocking it askew.

Drought comes, disease comes, late freezes, midsummer blizzards, cruel winters. Each time, nature returns, reshaped. Evolution happens here; the history of the earth is made here.

I like to think that I may still be able to struggle in and up to Two Ocean Plateau when I am old, and see a big brown pile of grizzly bear scat, and hear those wolves sing.